CW00392154

This is the work
places and incid   :
the author's imagination or are used fictitiously.
Any resemblance to actual persons, living or
dead, events, or locales is entirely coincidental.

The only exception of the above is the poem
Semerwater, My Best Friend and Beggars
Bridge, mentioned in My Little Dream Cottage.

First paperback editions March 2024

Book designed by author

ISBN 978-1-7394962-1-0 (paperback)
ISBN 978-1-7394962-0-3 (ebook)

For Mum —

Thank you for inspiring me to write my first poem
and the many others that followed.

I am dedicating this book to you with all my love.

Contents

The Clock*

Tick tick tick tick goes the clock.
Tick tick tick tock ticks the clock.
Tick tick tick,
Tock tock tick,
we hear the tick tick of the clock.

* My first poem, written between six and seven years old

A New Day

The mists from the river are swirling, seeping
and weeping over land,
bathing in the morning sunlight.
Oh, that freshness of a new day!
The dew on the grass,
humidity of mingling smell of water, sun and grass,
the faint aroma of burning wood.

Oh, the joy of the birth of another day!
The shrill sound of a dawn chorus
is a beauty that reaches within you,
so uplifting a morning can be.
All the people in the world, they can share in this moment.
So take comfort in a bond so beautiful,
that we can rejoice and sing with a coming of a new day.

Daisies of White and Gold

Delicate daisies
pure and white,
pretty petals
gently nodding in the light.

Sweet and innocent,
soft and fine,
little faces bathing in sunshine.

Petals of white,
hearts of gold
dancing in fields of old.

Almond-shaped vessels,
paper-thin,
catching raindrops upon
their delicate skin.

A field laced with tiny
heads of brilliant white,
subtle and divine
in a ray of sunlight.

A time to embrace
their simple beauty
so intricately refined,
so perfect to find.

The Forgotten Bridge

A lonely structure stands alone,
weathered bricks built of stone,
beneath a whirling, swirling river,
an arch standing on its own.

They built this bridge of stone,
graced ancestors unknown:
farmer, tailor, butcher, sailor.
Whispered ghosts, now passersby.
vanish into tombs nearby.

An eighteen-century production,
then a human construction,
a future direction to last.
Still beauty in that forgotten
bridge of the past.

Attachments

Letting go of defences
awakens your senses.

Free your mind of trials and trouble.
Let them float away in a bubble.

Blue Nose

Mr Frost is back again
scattering white lace
across the window pane.

Shivering in our beds,
woolly hats on our heads,
freezing fingers,
numb toes,
no heating —
just a blue nose.

Get up get up,
you'll be late for school!

Who wants to go to school
on a freezing cold day?
Only me, a silly old fool!

With freezing fingers
and numb toes
I drag my body
with my cold, blue nose.

Up too slow to eat
my pancake treat
in my nice warm seat.

On with my coat,
shoes on my feet,
off we go into icy sleet.

Freezing fingers,
numb toes.
sniffling through
a cold, blue nose.

Sisters' Tiff (A Child's Poem)

Cold, cold, cold!
Feeling ice-cold,
grab my jumper
and woolly socks!
Drink my hot chocolate
to warm me up.
Sweet, syrupy treat.
Sup, sup, sup,
mmmmmmm —
that tastes good!
Mmmmmmmmmmmmmm!

Silly sister Suzy
mimics me.
Heat rushes to my cheeks.
I push her off her seat!

Silly sister Suzy
crying madly
jumps to her feet,
just about to hit me.

I run off before she beats me,
leaving sister Suzy
crying hysterically.
Heard her from Timbuktu and back again,
That will teach her
not to mimic me!

On my Own on a Desolate Moor

I'm waiting on my own
on a lonely moor
for the bus to take me
to my nice, warm home.

It's spitting, nearly raining,
wind cool against my skin.
It rushes down the valleys,
shaking the shelter I'm in.

I'm feeling on my own.
Hurry up, bus, hurry up!
A passing walker
struggles against the wind.
He waves his hand,
turns around and grins
as he fights against
the rain and the wind
on this rugged moorland,
heading towards
The Old Windy Inn.

I'm feeling on my own.
Hurry up, bus, hurry up!
Shivering now,
I snuggle against
the shelter's plastic sheets,
precious little cover from
the wind and rain and sleet.

My attention is drawn
to blades of grass
tossing and wind-swept
on this desolate land.
The sheep are bleating
but no one's here to listen
to their fearful cries,
only me waiting,
sleet on my knees,
waiting for a bus,
rubbing my hands
in zero degrees,
teeth chattering
in the freezing breeze.

Before I see it, I hear
a distant sound of an engine,
a low hum and a rumble
trundling up the hill.
Then there upon the horizon,
the lights of a welcoming bus,
chugging through the foggy rain
with hardly even a fuss!

I release a final sigh,
a white mist of warm air,
into the chilly atmosphere,
wiping away one solitary tear.

Suddenly out of the mist it appears,
pulls up before me
on that desolate moor.
As the door opens free
the light and warmth
flood towards me.

'Where you going, miss?'
'To Whitby,' I say. 'Is this the right bus?'
'Yes, miss. Hop aboard,
sorry we're late.
The weather's not been too great.'

I pay my fare
and head up the stairs.
The bus rocks and chugs all the way there
but I don't mind
sitting on my own
because it's taking me back
to my nice, warm home!

A Smile

How important is a smile?
A smile can make us smile.
Crinkled eyes,
a delightful surprise!

Cheerfulness,
togetherness,
being just us.

Smile at someone today
and brighten up their day.
The world's a better place
with a smile upon your face.

Dress with style,
run a mile,
walk down an aisle,
take a cruise on the Nile
but — but remember never smile
at a crocodile!

Ripples

When we think of ripples
what comes to mind
is water moving in waves
peaceful and calm,
hypnotic crests and troughs.

Or sequential waves
sending messages
across rivers, ponds,
lochs and lakes
for curious minds to discover,
waves caused by a stone
thrown by an innocent lover
or a slight breeze
gently calling from noble trees.

Clear ripples of nature
for a stranger's eyes to see,
moving, gentle waves
that flow and break free,
rising and falling, spread out wide,
reflecting back the world outside,
circles of life, a constant flow,
a reminder that everything will come and go.

A Rose

Rich in colour,
bought with love in mind,
delicate petals
beautifully defined.

My heart responds to the emotion
of a gift with such devotion.
Don't forget to send a rose!
See how their love for you
intentionally grows.

If Only

If only you could wave a magic wand
and make it happen,
wouldn't it be good?
If our babies could only count to ten,
an athlete could only win a gold,
a lonely person only make a friend.

If only a man could reach Everest
as easily as a plane takes to the sky!
If all the folk in the world could only read and write!
if everyone could only live forever!

Don't forget about the poor beggar
in need of food and warmth:
hold his hand and lead him off the streets,
feed him and give a home and shelter!

But one day
our babies *will* count to ten,
an athlete *will* win a gold,
a lonely person *will* make a friend,
the man *will* reach Everest,
everybody *will* read and write
and live for eternity.

And what about the beggar?
Hold his hand, lead him off the streets,
feed him and give him shelter forever.
It will be the perfect world.

It's all possible
What's stopping us?
If only.

Lily

A delicate lily in bloom,
standing tall, with perfect poise
radiating peace and beauty
a symbol of grace, hope, love and purity.
The aroma of its petals fills the room.

My Best Friend

Through trials and tribulations,
emotional ups and downs,
tears, anger, heartbreaks,
celebrations, births and moving towns —
one text from me, and she makes herself free,
She's always been there for me,
giving reassurance for my mistakes,
sympathy for bones that ache.

I wouldn't be without her —
she's the best!
I am so blessed.

She's funny,
beautiful,
loyal
and smartly dressed.
She likes her pampering:
hair, make-up, eyelash tints;
she's comfortable in her own skin.

We laugh, we cry,
we're sad to say goodbye.
A week, a month, a year can pass
but a bond so strong forever lasts
between a Lancashire and a Yorkshire lass.

Cotton Wool Clouds

I dream one day of touching a cloud
that floats aimlessly upon a mountainside.

In an endless sky of radiant blue
delicate clouds saunter through.
Watch those cotton wool clouds
cruising through life,
moving infinitely
like swans gliding magnificently.

They drift, they float, they exude
a simple strength of solitude.
They swirl and twirl,
floating on air, sharing a sense of magnitude.

Nobody owns cotton wool clouds.
Free from human intervention
they float above us with no intention,
just a voice that speaks of perfection,
lots of tiny particles of ice
in a sumptuous paradise.

Perfect crystals, crystal clear,
suspended in the atmosphere,
they shield us from sun and cold
with canopies bestowed,
beauty simplified,
swiftly expanding,
connecting the world,
freestanding,
moving in silence,
floating formations
commanding
the nations.

I dream one day of floating on a cotton wool cloud
looking down on a world so proud.

Kaleidoscope Heart

The moment you came into my life
it changed forever.
You made me see things in a very different way.
It changed my very being to this day.
Through your eyes, I once again saw beauty and
meaning all around,
leaving old patterns behind and discovering patterns of
new,
creating landscapes of kaleidoscope joy,
unveiling to me the very essence of life
through colours and ever-changing magical shapes,
beauty and light —
so special you see it only
through a kaleidoscope's eye.
You showed me the way through dazzling mosaics of
beads down a tunnel of hidden gems,
escalating an intoxicating sense of freedom, a zest for
life's intention,
dazzling pieces of soothing bliss,
the warm whispers of a kiss,
the ever-changing patterns side by side.
A life's journey rich in tapestry
changing tides upon tides,
opening my mind to limitless possibilities,
a flicker of a dream then,
now an abundance of
happiness and passion,
qualities I had longed forgotten,
the patterns of kaleidoscope joy.

Carry this instrument in your subconscious mind
and every day you will see new shapes
of magical colour and design,
wonderment evolving in and around you,
an aura of vivid imagery to view.
You opened my eyes to a bright, new world.
Thank you for showing me the colourful light,
opening my mind to my new beautiful
kaleidoscope art.
I love you with all my heart.

Countryside

Standing so high, not a care
in the world, I see
wide open spaces of green places,
blue satin ribbons, streams so clean,
birds flying high that make my heart sigh,
gentle rising hills that have no frills,
breathtaking
clean air.

Standing so high, not a care
in the world, I see
land with green places of open spaces,
streams like ribbons in rippling blues.
Hearts sigh as birds fly high,
no frills with gentle hills —
just peace, tranquillity and outstanding views.

Floating Petals

Floating petals gently floating on a breeze,
Softly they dance gently they sway,
Delicately landing on the floor.
Making the finest carpet of petal decor.

As they drift and gently fall,
whispering tales as they all
rustle in the gentle wind.
A tale of beauty,
A tale of grace,
A reminder of life's gentle pace.

An Eagle's Eye

Way up high
an eagle's eye view.
Rivers merging,
Blue ribbons surging,
swelling, waves emerging,
seen from here
high in the sky.

Distant scene
of patchwork green,
twisting ripples
in between.
Tiny minnows,
whispering willows—
all catch the eye
of the eagle up high.

Narrow rows
of stone-built walls
meeting at a crossroads.
Jumping frogs,
croaking toads
where the river flows—
all seen by that knowing eye
of an eagle flying so high.

Velvet Brown

Smooth brown to the touch,
glossy coat of sheer sheen,
fragile legs like little sticks,
She walks so low to the ground.
She's a miniature Dachshund
Wide eyes of hazel green.
A bounce,
a toughness,
an annoying stubbornness:
Determined not to change her mind.
She's loyal,
she's double trouble;
mischievous
but always ready for a snuggle.

Her coat is like velvet
which reflects her name
although she thinks she's a Great Dane.
She has airs and graces,
holds her head high,
nose in the air.
She doesn't care at all.

Given a voice
she would have a lot to say
I'm sure.
You can't ignore a bark
that reaches right down to the park,
echoes around the place and travels right back again.

She's our little sausage and fourteen now.
She limps just a titch and can't even see a little bit.
She struggles with a few troubles
but give her a stick
she will show you her trick,
leaving us joyfully clapping and
every time a hit.
She chases it around,
catches it with her tail behind,
throws it right through
the open window
leaving us spellbound.

A special dog like no other,
she's our Velvet,
Velvet Brown.
She's unique
She deserves the Golden Crown.

She sleeps in a pink bed of fluff,
staring out in a warm daze
and doesn't want to leave it nowadays.
You have to drag her out,
tempt her with her favourite treat
(something nice to eat)
to get her off her warm fluffy seat.

She's our favourite,
we spoil her more and more
 every passing day.
 Hopefully, she'll grow stronger
and spread her warmth for longer.
She's our Velvet,
our very own Velvet Brown
who deserves the best of all the Golden Crowns.

Spring

Let the crocuses sing
their colour of delights
to warm up our hearts,
rich in purples, yellows and whites.
Let the sunshine
warm our faces,
make us feel human
once again after cold days
of winter's malaise.

Tiny buds on trees
that gently sway in the midnight breeze,
that test the time of wind rain and a cold December freeze.
A beauty simplified ready to shower
our skies with pinks and white petals to warm our heart's
desire.
The moonlight in dazzling white
appears on a quiet still night,
a moon that shines so very bright.

A dawn chorus
once again comforts us within,
blackbirds, robins and thrushes
chirping and cheeping
seeing the day in,
waking up to another morning,
striking beauty in vast oceans,
dazzling array of bewildering emotions,
blissfulness bliss, joyfulness joy,
a life blessed with the coming of another day!
Beauty in flowers, sunshine, birds and trees,
moonlight, sunlight, words and bees.

Celebrate the coming of another day,
our heart's embrace a fresh spring,
Go forth! Shout out from the depths of your heart!
Sing, sing, sing with the delights of a bright new spring!

The Storm

Driving through the winding roads,
the sky a translucent white,
Moving clouds hiding beams of angel light
Suddenly, a gust of wind, rain and sleet
surprises us in our warm, cosy seats.

Slashing rain hits the car
Like waves crashing down
on a boat about to sink
Echoes of voices, *Abandon ship!*
Alarmed, I fear steering down the street
through the wind, rain and sleet.

It's hard to concentrate.
I fear a freak storm in spate,
trees tangled wildly,
dancing in a frenzied state.
The sky turned to black.

Lightning flashes. Seconds pass.
We hear thunder crack!
My heart misses a beat.
I can't see out......
awash with spray of sleet, rain and wind,
wishing it would end.

At last an eerie calm bathes the land,
revealing through the glass
an expanse of blue sky.
The storm has passed!

Relief to see,
a fleeting glance,
home sweet home,
far in the distance.
I can breathe again,
relax in my seat,
hope we don't repeat
a storm of wind, rain and sleet
where my heart once missed a vital beat!

Be kind

Spread kindness like the
sunshine bright,
Every day and every night.
A simple smile, a gentle word,
May your heart sing like a
sweet humming bird,
Be helpful, be caring, be true,
The world needs more
kindness, and that can start
with you.

My Little Dream Cottage

I would love to have a little cottage one day
near Beggars Bridge, maybe a mile or two away,
just in the country
with a slate, stone roof,
with a sweet plum tree
and a marmalade cat
called Robinson Jack.

A cottage garden filled with
black-eyed Susans,
begonias, daisies and lilies
rich in purples, pinks and yellows
spilling out into pasture-rich meadows.

A garden wall of Yorkshire stone
encasing a sweet cottage home
with a marmalade cat called
Robinson Jack
basking in a nice sun trap
when one day, a robin lands smack
in front of the feline's nose.

Jack crouches on his four-legged toes
ready to pounce.
Unaware of the feline's steely gaze
the robin flies off
into the sunny haze
leaving poor old Jack
in a wee dizzy daze.

Watering my plants and picking plums for a very fine pie
to taste with my afternoon tea,
 under my sweet plum tree

Pink plant pots of marigolds, tiger lilies and begonias,
a garden filled with sweet aromas,
rich in foxgloves and lupins,
Delicately poised with butterfly wings,
pansies, peonies and peppermint leaves.

Pink clematis frames the white wooden door,
the prettiest blossom you will ever adore.
Take pleasure in this beautiful decor
before those pink petals float to the floor!

A pantry kitchen
with cotton curtains
to hide the pots, pans and tins.
Dark-beamed wooden ceilings
in a cosy cottage lounge
with an open fire that whistles and sings
tiled in a fancy pattern surround.
A rocking chair with a knitted cushion
donated by my old Aunt Susan
looking out of my sash windows
across my pretty garden
rich in purples, pinks and yellows
spilling out into pasture-rich meadows.

That's my dream of my little cottage one day
near Beggars Bridge, maybe a mile or two away.
A beautiful colour of plants galore,
an array of sweet perfumed petals
just in the country on a Yorkshire moor
with a slate stone roof,
with a sweet plum tree
and a marmalade cat
called Robinson Jack.

Mrs Molly Bluff It

Mrs Molly Bluff It
tried as she would
to sell her yellow buckets.
Little old Mrs Molly Bluff It
tried as she would
to sell her yellow buffets,
Mrs Molly Bluff It.
As you can see,
Her favourite colour is yellow
to attract her customers
in the market of Portobello.
Although good-natured,
she hoodwinks
honest lovely folk,
flogging her distinct
buckets and buffets.

As she tells a hearty casual joke
she is smart as she is vocal,
not an honest word
as she sells outside her local,
not a blink of an eye,
not a sorrowful sigh
as she sells her buckets and buffets
on a hot day in July.

Mrs Molly Bluff It
is used to idle gossip,
telling a joke or two
as she heartily
hoodwinks
a bloke or two
with her yellow buffets and buckets
in the market of Portobello Road;
with a mouthful of golden nuggets
looks right through you
as she says a quid or two will do.
Aye-aye, she says
with a wink of an eye
as she greets
her regular folk.

It's a shame she keeps a good man broke.
But always sells it with a hearty joke,
rich as a pauper can be
Looks can deceive
as she hides behind
her yellow buffets and buckets
but what gives it away
is her mouthful of nuggets.

We secretly agree Mrs Molly Bluff It
is as rich as the King and Queen,
selling her yellow buffets and buckets,
happy as the cat that got the cream
at a stall down this street in London
called Portobello Green.

Semerwater

To the eye, it's wonderful—

a beautiful basin of blue,
radiant azure, royal cobalt
shimmering through.
What a wonderful blue!
Its mammoth shape takes your breath away.
It's different,
it's unique.
There's nothing like its timeless mystique.
What a wonderful view
hidden amongst gentle hills
rising above the glorious site of radiant
blue.

Sui generis Semerwater will rest in peace in all its glory,
forever nestled in a valley to tell its story
to loyal disciples, onlookers, and gentlefolk.
It's alluring, appealing,
exquisitely bewitching,
gazing deeply at the wonderful view
in that beautiful basin
of timeless blue.

Sui generis is Latin for 'unique'

Sincerity

We should never underestimate the power of sincerity,
a smile, a touch, a warm embrace
making the world a better place.
A heart-felt emotion,
so pure and innocent,
unlike a stinging bumble bee.
Sincerity is what will finally set us free.

Daffodils

As the winter days pass,
the smell of spring awakens us
to see the delicate petals unfold
into beautiful colours of petals gold.

They bring us happiness,
they bring us joy.
Oh, to see them dancing and shivering
in the whispering breeze
Yellow crowns with tailored flutes
standing upon their unstable roots.

Flowers dancing and shivering
in the whispering breeze
but gone so quickly, golden flowers,
that bring us joy until next Spring!

Manners

Manners cost nothing.
Every day it's just what's done.
Manners matter to everyone.
A simple 'thank you' can change the world,
making it a better place for anyone.
When it comes to signs of respect,
it can be a sign of intellect.
It matters a great deal.
So please say 'thank you' and don't forget.
It's time to appreciate
what others create
for you to shine
so don't miss out on your best moment in time.
An attitude that's courteous and polite
will go down well and be received with delight.
See the results to your self-esteem.
Your insecurities will finally rest
and you will be at your very best.
Please don't hurt others by lacking respect.
Put yourself in their shoes that now feel regret.
Turn it around.
It's never too late to say
a simple 'thanks' for not
seeing them upset.
Make it fair —
just two small words
to show that you care
for the world,
that loving place
we all have to share.

Miracle Machine

Clouds moving graciously in the sky,
a gathering crowd looking up high,
a moving object made of steel so bright,
hands shielding screwed up eyes to light.
A roar, a clap of thunder shaking the world with wonder.

3…. 2 ….. 1! Launch already, a forgotten number!
A sight to man, an awe-inspiring moment
to see metal so bright awash the earth with so much light.
A rocket at speed devouring vast space
racing into the unknown at such a fast pace
with power, noise, light, and chase.
Then
silence.
Nothing.
Gone
in a flash leaving a trail of vapour,
millions of tiny droplets evaporating
in front of hungry eyes
still looking up high now into empty skies.
A wondrous sight is gone forever,
a once-in-a-lifetime moment to treasure.

Life on a Canvas

Shifting colours upon a crystal gaze,
Beauty in a fiery, red sunset ablaze,

Changing colours of Autumn hue
Winter's chill tinged with blue.

A picture of all seasons to embrace,
Moving hearts of desire in one place.
Feelings stir in wondrous space
Of colour, beauty and honest grace.

Life blooms in a lotus flower,
Sweetly scented petals of white, pink and blue
Drifting on an island green,
Reflecting strength in purity,
Symbolic, rebirth, divine beauty.

Ever-changing seasons in one place
Filled with colours of life in a silent space,
Painting pictures on a canvas,
Brush strokes with a turn and a twist.
Sun-kissed scenes
create moments of bliss
Through reflective eyes of an unknown artist.

At a Crossroads

At a crossroads, nowhere to go,
no place to call my own.
No sharing memories, emotions
and love. Stuck.
Living in solitude and emptiness.

I crave to be fulfilled with the love
that I know will come.
But 'when' and 'where'
are the questions I keep asking.

What is this place?
It is the Crossroads.
Why, oh why does life throw
these paths our way

when all we want
is an easy road?
Do we have to learn more?
Why does it have to be so hard?
Because we have to make choices,
And those choices made, we hope,
will lead to our beautiful life of destiny.

So please do not fear the crossroads.

Acknowledgements

There are a few people I would like to thank.
First, I would like to thank Helena Nelson
who edited my poems beautifully and kept me on track.

Thank you to my friends Lisa Watch, Claire Bennett
and Aisha Cunningham for their support and
encouragement.

Thank you to my family for just being there.

Finally, I must thank my mother, who has always been
my greatest fan and inspiration. From the day she sat
me down as a six-year-old girl and said we are going to
write a poem. That was the day I never looked back,
and has brought me to this destination today.

Thank you, my dearest mother,
Valerie Jackson MBE.

Printed in Great Britain
by Amazon

43479753R00030